TWO LETTERS TO CYPRUS

Germanus II
Ecumenical Patriarch of Constantinople

Translated by: D.P. Curtin

Copyright @ 2020 Dalcassian Press

All rights reserved. No part of this publication may be reproduced, distributed, or transmitted in any form or by any means, including photocopying, recording, or other electronic or mechanical methods, without the prior written permission of the publisher, except in the case of brief quotations embodied in critical reviews and certain other non-commercial uses permitted by copyright law. For permission request, write to Dalcassian Press at dalcassianpublishing at gmail.com

ISBN: 979-8-3302-6308-0 (Paperback)

Library of Congress Control Number:
Author: Curtin, D.P. (1985-)

Printed by Ingram Content Group, 1 Ingram Blvd, La Vergne, Tennessee

First printing edition 2020.

TWO LETTERS TO CYPRUS

TWO LETTERS TO CYPRUS

LETTER I

The most holy Patriarch of Constantinople, Germanus, sent a letter to the island of Cyprus, both from himself and from the holy synod, when Lord Neophytus held the chief office of the priesthood on that island and was being forced to submit to the Latins.

1. The island of Cyprus, that famous one, which is surrounded on all sides by the clear mouth of the sea, but is proclaimed by the fiery tongues of orators and writers, enjoying a convenient location and good weather as if the sea surrounding the island of Cyprus is rich in good things, and in a barren place it pours forth sweet juice from salty soil, another land of the blessed, a land dripping with milk; which not only pours forth all fertility from itself, but also becomes filled with external goods, as many as are brought into it through its waters.

2. Moreover, this very Cyprus, once happy and splendid, was not so remarkable for its natural gifts, as the discourse has already shown, nor was anything else distinguished it from others so much as the fruit of piety itself, and the harvest of the Gospel, bearing a hundredfold of good grains, as abundant streams of teachings flow, and a flourishing meadow of Scriptures, and a multitude of Church sons like various herbs of the field; like a renewed island, as Scripture speaks, and daily renewed and progressing for the better. Hence it happened that it was promoted to one of the greatest provinces, and raised to the dignity of an archbishopric, becoming an exceptional lot of Christ, and directing its own flock under its shepherds.

3. But it was not the wicked Satan's wish to look upon this without envy, who threatens to destroy the land and the sea. Certainly, he arms barbaric hands, and rouses an enemy nation against the Church, indeed a beneficent one; a nation that devours with teeth, tears with claws, and tramples with feet, utterly devastating everything towards destruction, according to Daniel's vision. For the Latins, even the Cypriots have been attacked: a certain immense sea and all that lies in its path, surrounding the island with its conspicuous waves; indeed, it does not seek to cover it, but is confined within its own boundaries,

breaking the waves within itself, and yielding to the providence of the Creator.

4. The audacity of the Italians crosses its own boundaries, and it rolls the waves of anger, runs outside the limits, and attacks outsiders. Such a fierce storm was stirred up in the renowned Cyprus; with which the sea keeps its pact, and the wave returns to its calm. Indeed, this flood corrupted everything more beautiful for a certain time, and it laid low whatever was standing tall on the land. Soon, it also touched the bodies of men. Nevertheless, the calamity was tolerable, although it was very severe; because it pertained to bodily harm, and the destruction of bodies. A short time later, they are gathered and soon dissolved. But now, the situation has proudly lifted itself against the souls and tries to shake the right discourse of piety. For along with the Latin warriors, not a few priests of the same kind entered the island, disturbed the Churches, and insolently tried to drag all divine things to themselves.

5. Hence, the legitimate and canonical first of the shepherds, the most blessed Archbishop of the Cypriots, Lord Neophytus, was driven from his seat. Moreover, a certain newcomer and a man of a foreign tongue, of Latin descent, sitting on the same throne, asserts that he will not allow himself to be ruled by any other reason, except that our sacred men, both bishops and others, should feed and teach the Roman or Greek people, unless they have first submitted to their subjection and provided pleasing agreements to the new and unworthy pontiff; otherwise, they should be completely expelled from the island, so that with the shepherds and teachers dispersed, there is a danger that Christ's flock may wander into precipices and chasms.

6. And indeed, these things had long been circulated and had reached the ears of our mediocrity. But now, the most religious Leontius, the most holy bishopric of Sole in Cyprus, and the reverend supervisor of the monastery of Apsinthiorum, the priest monk Leontius, sent to our mediocrity, both by their most blessed archbishop and the other bishops, not to mention the entire sacred assembly and the people themselves, reported these synodical calamities before our mediocrity; and today, presenting them in the midst, they spoke on behalf of the embassy that had been entrusted to them by those people. They said that it was by no means allowed by the Latins for Archbishop Neophytus to remain on the island in that way, as the other archbishop of theirs would in no way tolerate another archbishop. Therefore, they

completely expelled him, and now he wanders through the regions of the East.

7. The envoys added that the Pontiff of the Latins compels the bishops themselves and all the sacred order to submit, and promises to allow them to have their own bishoprics under that condition, and to perform sacred duties. Then they begged us and the sacred brotherhood to learn what should be done from us. For they said that the souls of all the Cypriots were present through their language, and embraced the knees of our mediocrity, and begged us humbly to take care of their salvation, and not to leave a region so vast and populous without protection, so that it may not hunger and suffer thirst, not from lack of food and drink, but from not hearing the word of God.

8. When the bishop prayed humbly, and the abbot pleaded, our community along with the holy brotherhood proposed to deliberate. It seemed that a twofold danger was imminent on both sides, and a hasty outcome from each side. For indeed, to abandon the people without pastoral protection, whose blood must be sought by God from the hands of the shepherds, is a sin deserving of great condemnation: but to yield to the will of the Latins, and make a covenant with the schismatics, seems discordant with the strictness of the canons, and foreign to the ecclesiastical customs. Therefore, the debate was uncertain, and inclining towards either side was doubtful. But after our community and the holy brotherhood had pondered many considerations, finally our community decided that the very appearance of subjection demanded by the Latins should be presented to the synod. Thus, it encouraged the bishop and the abbot to explain spiritually and truthfully what those things were that were being demanded by the Latins.

9. They replied that these three things must inevitably be demanded in Latin: first, to join hands with hands, priestly matters with priestly matters, our Latin affairs with Latin ones; for this is a safe precaution against hostile actions in servile matters of relaxation; secondly, that a Roman, to be promoted to a priestly honor, after being elected by his people, whether he is promoted to bishop or to another ordination or appointed to a monastic prefecture, should not be established in a dignity pertaining to him without the knowledge of the Latins. The Latins have only contested that they seek this for shameful gain. Thirdly, they added to this, that the Greeks, by their own bishops,

should be judged when necessary; however, if someone from those judged should perhaps want to appeal to the Latin archbishop, as if oppressed, whether he be a cleric or a layman, let the dispute be settled by him. Our mediocrity, after discussion with the congregation of brothers, and with a definitive decree initiated, and also declaring what seemed fitting, pronounced in this manner.

10. We have already decreed, relying on the grace of Christ, to embrace and preserve unharmed and inviolate all sacred canons, divine traditions, and all the venerable and most pious rites of our Church. Indeed, we have written and confessed this, and every day we contend for them, and we pray that the hand and voice of the patriarch Jacob may stand firm, who was beloved by God even before he was born. However, if there is any abdication of canons, traditions, rituals, the faith itself, if anything that the bishops of Cyprus may have been able to carry out intentionally and without causing offense to the Church of Christ, and if they have supported and freed their churches from what truly appears to be falling away, causing them to truly decline, I believe that forgiveness should be granted in this economy or dispensation, or to speak more truly, in this simulation; and they will be considered free from fault, as those who have the great Paul as their patron in that matter.

11. Therefore, after our judgment of mediocrity was pronounced in this way, when at that time there was a considerable part of the students from Constantinople, divided into three groups, namely clerics, monks, and laypeople; some of whom had already been driven out from there and were hated for their perfect love and confession towards the heavenly Father, adorning themselves with their sweat and toil; while others, like weaned children, had returned to their mother (I mean this city of Constantine), and were still being supported by her old and needy arms; such people, fervent in heart with burning coals of zeal, breathing out fire, using sharp voices, were arguing against us.

12. Saying: Let your light shine before men, not only through your deeds, but also through your very words; and let nothing dark or obscure be hidden in your decrees. From what we have suffered, we have learned the deceits of the Latins. We have had more than enough dealings with them, endured much hardship, persevered in prisons, expelled from our homeland, subjected to disgrace in our beards; and

from all these things, we have been fully taught their deceptions. The Latins speak one thing, but hide another in their minds. They demand that our hands be joined with theirs, asserting that this is entirely without fault or blame; when in fact, it is nothing but a betrayal of the faith handed down by our ancestors, and a guidance towards showing obedience to their Church, and towards all the complete delusions that are practiced in senile Rome.

13. For as those who have always been involved in wars, and who are all clearly devoted to Mars, both laymen and their priests, and who are well acquainted with the institutions of wars, they consider the act of joining hands as a sign of defeat and complete servitude: just as those do in battles who have been overcome. We therefore urge that this be expressly included in the synodal decrees, so that the hands of the Cypriots are not handed over to the Italians; even though the matter may not have seemed worthy, for which mention would be made in the sacred canons. For if this is not done, there is a clear danger that the strong and blameless structure of the pontiffs who preceded you, which they built with much sweat and long labors, may soon collapse, strengthening us daily with their admonitions, and stabilizing us on the foundation of the apostles, so that we may not fear the rivers and winds of temptations.

14. When the most devout people standing there followed with fervent zeal our mediocrity presiding over the synod, seeing our mediocrity, that here economic reasoning would help nothing, but rather cause turmoil; and that not only would it not tend towards the right itself to save the famous Cyprus already shipwrecked, while according to nautical laws, it brings back the foot, and loosens the wet sail; but there would also be a danger that it would compel the carriers of our own ship to rebellion; and as if external pirates were not enough for harassment, it would openly be feared that they would engage themselves in conflict with each other, the partners of the navigation; these words were spoken to the Cypriots: Christ's mouthpiece Paul, through my mouth, pronounces judgment, and responds to your question as follows: I urge you, brothers, to watch out for those who cause dissensions and stumbling blocks, contrary to the teaching you have received; and turn away from them, for they do not serve Christ the Lord, but their own wickedness; and through sweet words and blessings they deceive the hearts of the innocent. This defense is

entirely sufficient for us, and it is very relevant to the question, and it can abundantly teach what will be useful.

15. But you, brothers in Christ of Cyprus, are imitators of the Church of Constantinople; imitate its pastors who are the pastors of Cyprus, constantly blowing the trumpet of words, and attracting with exhortative and salutary songs. Let the flocks of Cyprus emulate the sheep of Constantinople, for these, although far removed from their shepherds, having common pasture with fierce wolves, having their woolly ornament shorn, and their flesh cut up, have kept the seal of faith safe from snares, and have rebuked the gaping wolves in vain. For if some of them, very few in number, have been partakers of some scab or even rabid bites, they truly ran to the resin in Gilead and to the spiritual physicians of this place; through whom they also returned to their former health, achieving no less praise than the unharmed and uninjured, for acknowledging their own weakness, and for seeking remedy swiftly.

16. Therefore, it may happen that the shepherds of Cyprus, when they encounter wolves, fighting for their flocks and caring for their safety, may falter a little and give way, God forbid. We urge them not to fall into despair immediately, not to abandon hope of salvation, not to join injustice with injustice, and not to progress for the worse, mingle with the nations, and learn their ways; but to immediately pick themselves up from the fall and seek a doctor. And this is how it should be.

17. As for the other two points, namely, that no one should be appointed to an inappropriate spiritual dignity without the knowledge of the Latins, and that the Romans, whether clergy or laity, should not be prevented from appealing to the Latins in cases of serious disputes, if they believe they are being wronged by the judges of their own people; these seem indifferent to our moderate stance, openly requested by the Latins solely for the sake of shameful profit. For indeed, they gain considerable profit from it. And our moderation advises the shepherds of Cyprus that whenever they encounter stubborn and contentious Latins driven by greed and profit, they should yield in those matters and not resist them. It is truly praiseworthy to gain spiritual profit at the expense of bodily harm, just as gold is exchanged for silver. Perhaps after their hands are filled with money, they will be absolved from the demanded hand tradition, and with their hands weighed down by the burden, they will be able to

raise holy hands to God, and celebrate sacred mysteries without deceit or bias.

18. These things having been taken from the daily notes of the synods and confirmed through the subscription and seal of the most revered and most holy guardian of the great Church of God, Chartophylax Theodoros Stilbe, were given in the month and indiction above written, in the year 6734.

LETTER II

The second letter of the same most holy lord Germanos to the Cypriots.

1. Most Christian men and lovers of piety, all of you who inhabit the renowned island of Cyprus, Romans and Syrians, all lovers of orthodoxy, careful guardians of the faith handed down to us by the Fathers, concerning which Christ, by the arm of the almighty God and Father, built His Church, and the gates of hell shall not prevail against it. For the more it is attacked, the more it is strengthened, exalting itself through the imitation of Christ. For His word is most true, when He says: "If they have persecuted me, they will also persecute you; if they have kept my word, they will keep yours also." Therefore, brothers, rejoice in the Lord always; and again I say, rejoice. Let your charity be inflamed and incited by the ascension of the brother of God, James, together with Paul, to spiritual struggles. Indeed, James says: "Count it all joy, my brothers, when you fall into various trials." Here, while he gladly boasts in his weaknesses, and takes pleasure in his tribulations.

2. I, certainly the least and most useless among the pontiffs, considered myself blessed in my weaknesses, because I have spoken to the most obedient people and to the ears of those who listen. For our word did not fall on rocky ground, nor did we write on water, nor did we cast our nets of doctrine in vain; but we sowed rather in good soil and fertile ears, we wrote in illuminated and pure hearts, with our tongue moved like the pen of that scribe mentioned in the Psalms; and having cast the net in the word of Christ, we led you to the obedience of faith, and we offered you as a heavenly feast worthy of Christ. Therefore, filled with joy at the first capture, and considering ourselves blessed because the purpose had succeeded, we once again lowered our tongue as a plow to the doctrine in the name of Christ.

3. By no means is it hidden from you, men most devoted to the studies of literature and disciplines, that our Fathers, who from the beginning were heralds of God and divine, moved by the divine Spirit, and following the apostolic doctrines, have arranged and determined all things pertaining to the Catholic Church in a spiritual distribution, according to the inspiration of God, and have surrounded them with boundaries, in accordance with various determinations of the Churches, and have enclosed each province everywhere for caution, so that the ambitious and arrogant ones would not easily leap from their

own to others; but fearing the walls of the most terrible excommunications and alienations from God, each cultivated the portion assigned to them, and were content with their own lot and inheritance.

4. But, oh my error-filled one, who has an insatiable ambition that rejects all canonical discipline in every way, and strives to overthrow every Christian institution, indeed even boldly leaps against the head of the Church itself, which is Christ, and does not fear the goads that Christ once threatened Saul with, saying to him: "It is hard for you to kick against the goads."

5. For we all know, who have been baptized with Christian baptism, that there is one master and guide for us, Christ, who is also the head of all Christians throughout the world; and all, honored with pontifical dignity, are brothers and members in the Church of Christ. And the truth indeed is this; Christ himself, who is the very truth, testifies, as do those who saw him and were his ministers. But the Italian arrogance does not want this, nor can it bear Christ to be the head and be called so; rather, rejecting Him from this order, it bestows him upon the senior pontiff of Rome; then it tries to revive the number of the quinaries of the patriarchate and make one of them, and dares to place his throne above the clouds, and liken him to the Most High. By clouds, I mean the lofty pontifical seats, high and destined in the patriarchate; through which all earthly things are exalted, receiving a voluntary and mystical shower of spiritual doctrine. Oh, how worthy of tears are these things, how worthy of groans! That spirit of pride, dark and the author of great sins, has conquered this race of men, full to overflowing.

6. Indeed, the first and greatest crime of the Italians is the addition of those forbidden to the Creed of Faith; so that it would never be attempted, they subjected to perpetual anathema those who dared to do so in an ecumenical and holy synod. Let him who wishes read the first canon of the Sixth General Synod, which ends verbatim as follows: But if anyone does not hold and embrace all the aforementioned decrees of piety, and thinks and preaches otherwise, but opposes them, let him be anathema according to the previously set forth declarations of the holy and blessed Fathers' decrees; and let him be cast out and expelled from the Christian community. For we have determined not to add anything or take away anything from what was

previously defined in any way we could. And this is the aforementioned canon. But that in every ecumenical synod, the pope of that time has through his vicars given consent to established dogmas and canons, no student of erudition is ignorant.

7. What can be gathered from this? The pontiffs of old Rome of this time do not accept and embrace those of old Rome, who lived in the times of the seven general councils of saints; but just as we reject and disregard the Greeks, they also reject and disregard them, as they do not accept what has been pronounced and confirmed by them synodically. So now the Italians are introducing a new faith and new dogma, and inventors of other canons. Therefore, they seek another Christ and other apostles. For those Fathers of the synods, inspired by the Divine Spirit, and heralds of God, did not at all believe in the Holy Spirit, who has existence from two persons, but they added faith to Christ, as in all other things. Even in matters concerning the Spirit, when He taught that He proceeds from the Father.

8. And these things I have briefly explained to your charity, so that you may understand how great an evil it is to subject oneself spiritually and obey the senior of Rome in special institutions: for I refrain from using harsher language. Therefore, I command all laypeople, who are genuine children of the Catholic Church, to completely avoid those priests who have submitted themselves to the obedience of the Latins: do not gather with them in the church, nor receive any blessings from their hands. For it is better to pray to God alone in your homes than to gather in the church with those who follow the Latin practices. However, if any of these priests lead an honest life, are well-mannered, and embrace piety, but only sin in that they have succumbed to the tyranny of the Latins who have invaded the churches there, and have professed to recognize the pope as their pontiff; let them not be allowed to come together with you in the church and perform priestly duties unless they have first converted, and in front of the Latin archbishop and bishops subject to him, said: "I will not act in this way anymore; but let the strength be in the synodal separation that was made before the Mass. And again, until they return to our divine and sacred synod and our moderation according to what that scripture contains.

9. And the clerics subject to them, as many as adhere to our Church, and wish to retain the faith handed down by the Fathers, are not

subject to their own pontiffs who demand obedience; nor if they, while obeying the Latin Church, are excommunicated by them, will they in any way care at all. For such a censure is null and void, rather it turns back on the censors; since they have also been the cause of scandals among the people of God, when they trampled upon the discipline of the sacred canons, welcomed invaders and seekers of foreign things, and gave them their hands, which is a sign of obedience and servitude, although they claim to say: We have not in any way betrayed our ancestral customs, nor have we done anything beyond the prescriptions of the sacred canons; they are ignorant of what they are saying. For the canons of the holy apostles and divine Fathers subject bishops who invade foreign regions to segregation; and they also subject them to anathema.

10. But you, the special people of Christ, stand firm, act manfully, be strengthened; restrain the disorderly, rebuke those who adulterate piety; not proclaiming any false teachings that you have received from the beginning; considering all the troubles of this life, and all the loss, joy, and gain, as long as the unviolated treasure of orthodox faith is preserved in you; which each one of us, carrying at the end of life, may depart from this world; indeed naked from all worldly things, and placing hope in this sole treasure, and expecting to hear that desirable voice: Your faith has saved you; go in peace; for which there is no limit or end.

11. May you all be kept safe by the almighty right hand of God, both Romans and Syrians, as many as are adorned with sacred dignity, and keep your minds free from that slavery which arises from the new deviation concerning faith, and as many as among the laity are fervent imitators of orthodoxy.

12. The grace of our Lord Jesus Christ, and the love of God and the Father, and the communion of the Holy Spirit, be with all of you. Amen.

The Scriptorium Project is the work of a small group of lay people of various apostolic churches who are interested in the preservation, transmission, and translation of the works of the early and medieval church. Our efforts are to make the works of the church fathers accessible to anyone who might have an interest in Christian antiquities and the theological, philosophical, and moral writings that have become the bedrock of Western Civilization.

To-date, our releases have pulled from the Greek, Syriac, Georgian, Latin, Celtic, Ethiopian, and Coptic traditions of Christianity, and have been pulled from sundry local traditions and languages.